Lakes & Rivers

Andrea Rivera

abdopublishing.com

Published by Abdo Zoom, a division of ABDO, PO Box 398166, Minneapolis, Minnesota 55439.
Copyright © 2018 by Abdo Consulting Group, Inc. International copyrights reserved in all countries.
No part of this book may be reproduced in any form without written permission from the publisher.
Launch!™ is a trademark and logo of Abdo Zoom.

Printed in the United States of America, North Mankato, Minnesota.

092017

012018

THIS BOOK CONTAINS
RECYCLED MATERIALS

Photo Credits: iStock, Shutterstock

Production Contributors: Kenny Abdo, Jennie Forsberg, Grace Hansen, John Hansen

Design Contributors: Dorothy Toth, Neil Klinepier

Publisher's Cataloging-in-Publication Data

Names: Rivera, Andrea, author.

Title: Lakes & rivers / by Andrea Rivera.

Other titles: Lakes and rivers

Description: Minneapolis, Minnesota: Abdo Zoom, 2018. | Series: Habitats |
    Includes online resource and index.

Identifiers: LCCN 2017939236 | ISBN 9781532120671 (lib.bdg.) | ISBN 9781532121791 (ebook) |
    ISBN 9781532122354 (Read-to-Me ebook)

Subjects: LCSH: Lakes--Juvenile literature. | Rivers--Juvenile literature. | Habitats--Juvenile literature.

Classification: DDC 577.6--dc23

LC record available at https://lccn.loc.gov/2017939236

Table of Contents

Lakes and rivers are freshwater habitats.

A lake is a still body of water.
A river flows.

Animals rely on these habitats for food and water. Some live in the water. Others live nearby.

Mammals like beavers can be found in rivers. **Reptiles** like turtles live in lakes and rivers.

Lots of **amphibians** and fish live in these habitats too.

There are more than 15,000 types of freshwater fish!

Technology

Rivers can provide power. The river's flow turns a **turbine** in a dam.

This powers a motor. The motor makes electricity. Power lines bring electricity to other places.

Engineering

Speedboats cruise on lakes. They are made to move fast! Engines power them.

Their shape helps them move easily over the water.

Art

There are many rocks at the bottoms of rivers and lakes.

Rock balancing
is a cool art form.
It takes a lot of
patience!

Math

Lake Baikal is in Russia. It is the deepest lake on Earth. It is about 5,371 feet (1,637 m) deep.

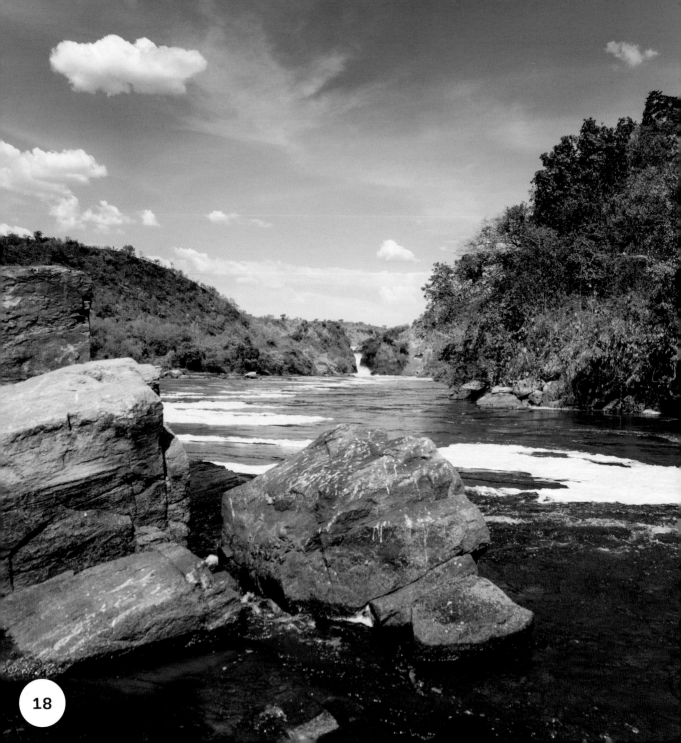

The Nile River is in Africa. It is the world's largest river. It is about 4,160 miles (1,267 m) long.

- The five Great Lakes are in North America. They are some of the world's biggest lakes. The Great Lakes have almost one-fifth of the world's surface fresh water.

- Antarctica is the only continent that does not have moving rivers and streams. All the water there is frozen.

- Sometimes rivers go over cliffs. This creates waterfalls.

Glossary

amphibian – a cold-blooded animal with a skeleton inside its body that hatches in water and breathes with gills. With age, it changes and develops lungs to breathe air and live on land.

mammal – a warm-blooded animal with fur or hair on its skin and a skeleton inside its body.

patience – the ability to stay calm when things take time.

reptile – a cold-blooded animal with a skeleton inside its body and dry scales or hard plates on its skin.

turbine – an engine with blades that turn by a force, such as moving water.

Online Resources

For more information on
lakes and rivers, please visit
abdobooklinks.com

Learn even more with the
Abdo Zoom STEAM database.
Visit **abdozoom.com** today!

Index